Sean Kenney

Cool Castles

Christy Ottaviano Books

Henry Holt and Company

New York

For Brian

Henry Holt and Company, LLC
Publishers since 1866
175 Fifth Avenue
New York, New York 10010
mackids.com

Library of Congress Cataloging-in-Publication Data
Kenney, Sean.
Cool castles / Sean Kenney.
   p.   cm.
ISBN 978-0-8050-9539-5 (hardcover)
1. Castles—Models—Juvenile literature. 2. LEGO toys—Juvenile
literature. 3. Military miniatures—Juvenile literature. I. Title.
U311.K46 2012   688.7'2—dc23   2012006045

First Edition—2012 / Book designed by Elynn Cohen
LEGO bricks were used to create the models for this book.
The models were photographed by John E. Barrett.
Printed in China by Toppan Leefung Printing Ltd.,
Dongguan City, Guangdong Province

10 9 8 7 6 5 4 3 2 1

Let's build a castle!

How to use this idea book

LEGO bricks give you the chance to build models! Follow the figures through their day to get ideas for things to make with pieces you have at home. There are instructions for a few models to get you started, but then see what you can build using your own imagination. It's okay if you don't have exactly the same pieces. Be creative and see if you can design something using what's in your LEGO collection.

All the models in this book were built using pieces from off-the-shelf LEGO products, including the Castle, Creator, and Harry Potter sets.

On the castle farm

It's a lot of work harvesting food for the king and queen.

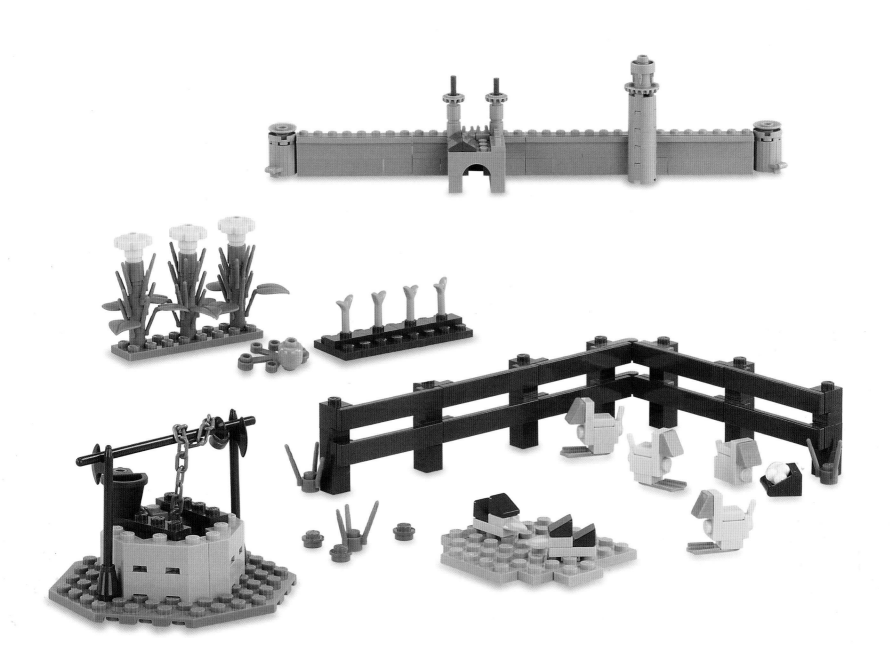

Four-legged help

Animals assist with the work. The stables are where they're fed and sheltered.

Add diagonal tiles to resemble timber-framed architecture.

1

2

Build some animals

Use regular pieces to build any kind of animal you can imagine.

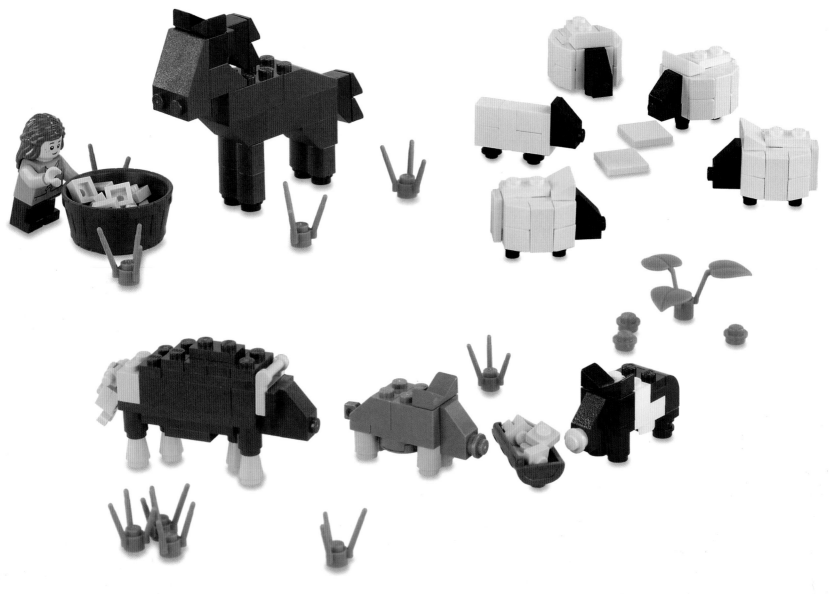

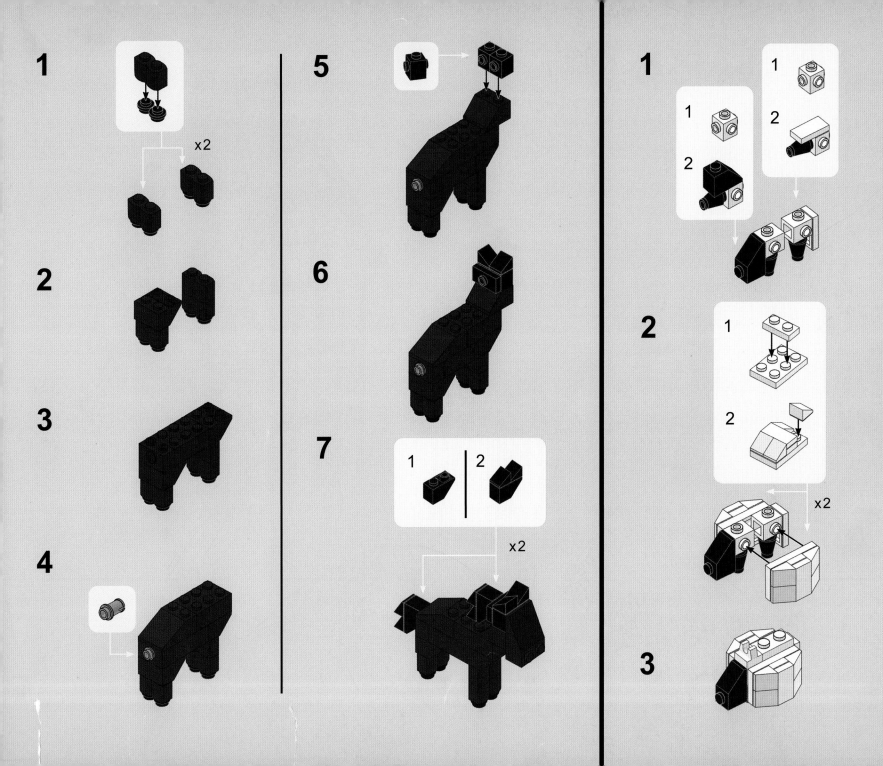

Let's head to town

There's lots to see and do in a medieval village.

Shopping at the market

Let's buy some fresh flowers,
food, drinks, and tools.

The castle looms over the village

Built of stone and wood, the castle protects the village from intruders.

15

Four chunks, endless combos!

Build your castle in separate sections, then combine them however you'd like.

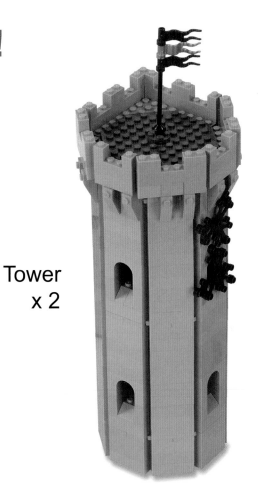

Tower
x 2

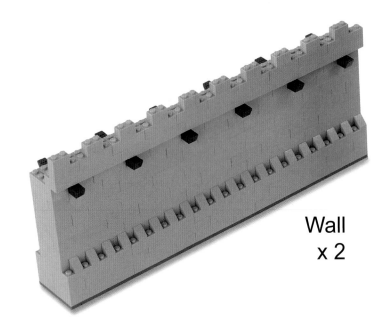

Wall
x 2

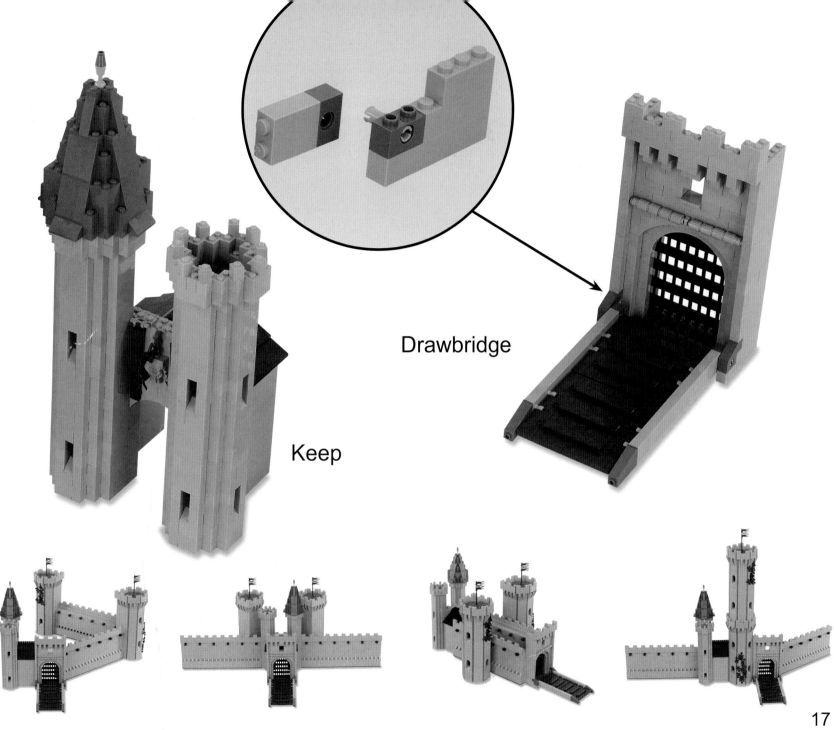

Keep

Drawbridge

17

Making circular towers

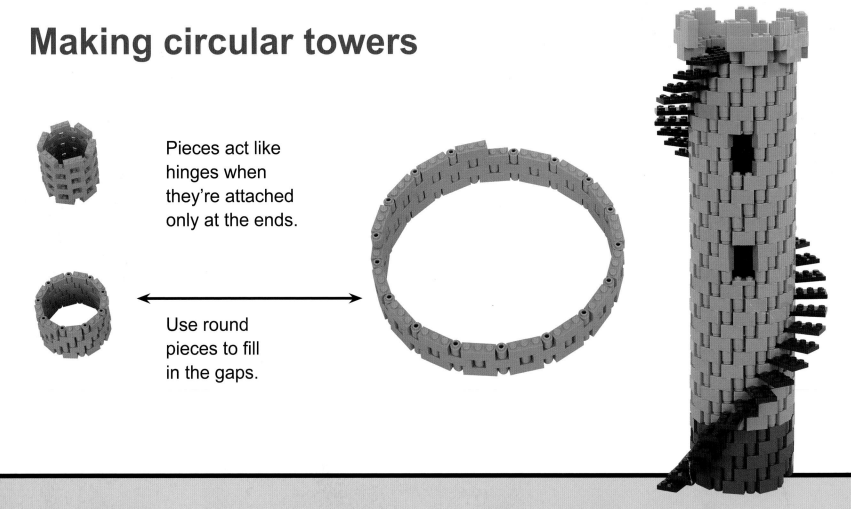

Pieces act like hinges when they're attached only at the ends.

Use round pieces to fill in the gaps.

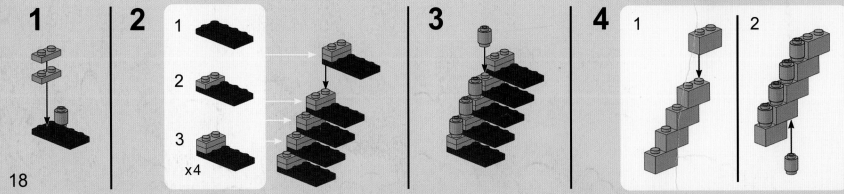

1

2

1

2

3

x4

3

4

1

2

Don't forget the details

Bricks

Chandelier

Windows

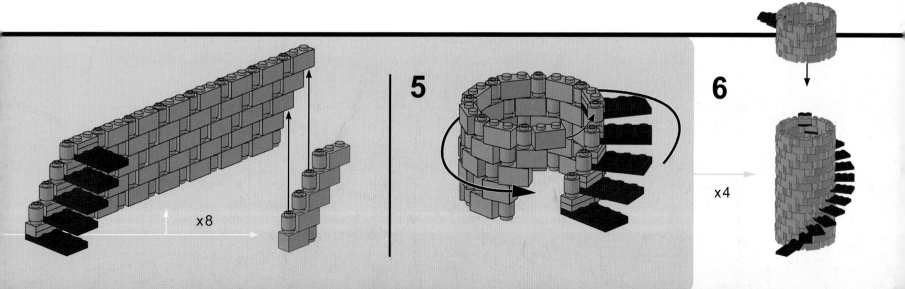

x8

5

6

x4

A kingdom from above

Build a miniature castle that stretches far and wide.

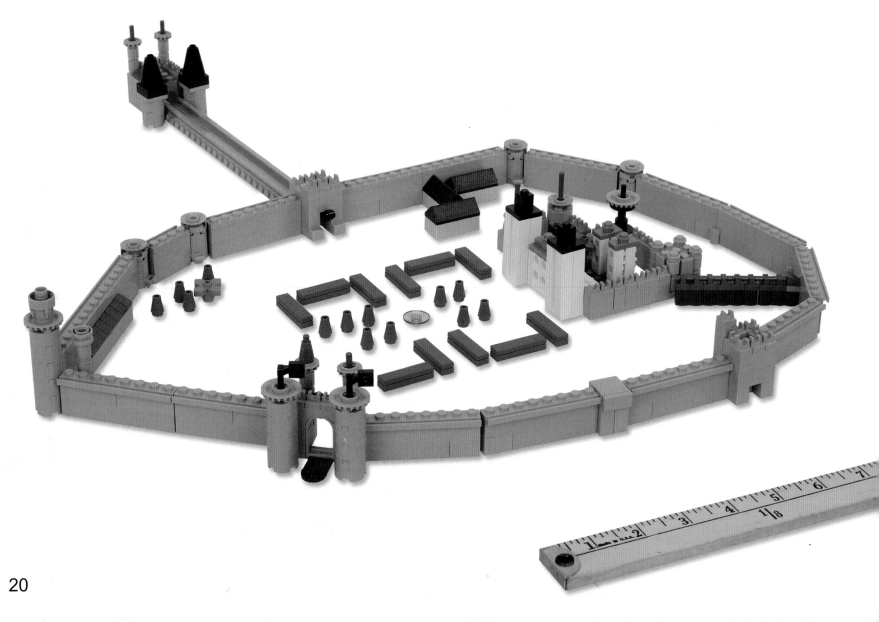

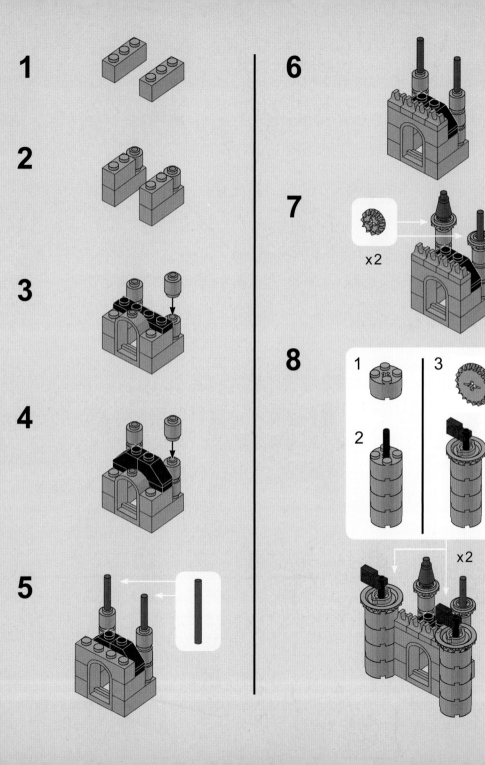

1

2

3

4

5

6

7 x2

8

1

2

3

x2

Time for a tournament

Life within the castle walls is so different from on the farm.

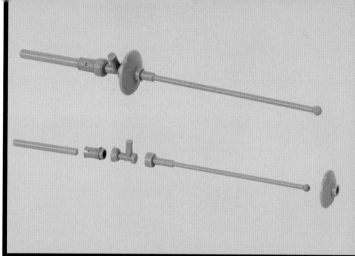
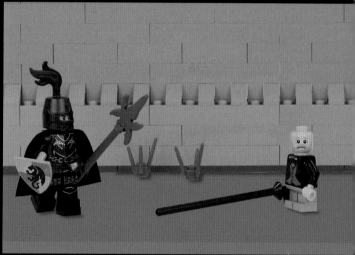

Oh no, dragon attack!

Deploy the castle defenses and save the kingdom from doom!

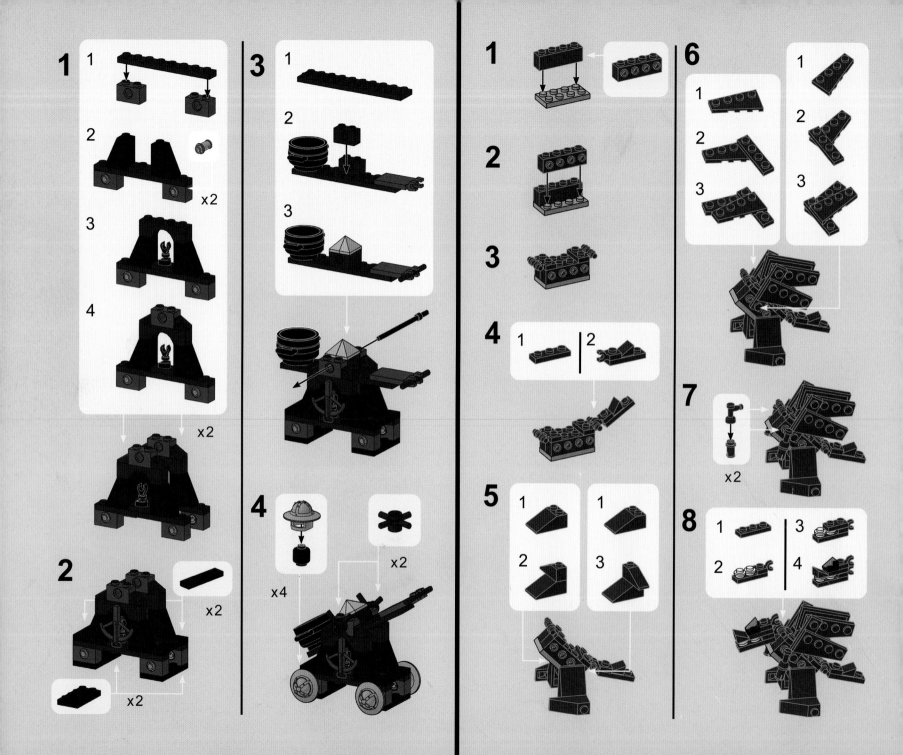

A dungeon so deep

Victory! Let's keep that rotten dragon locked up in the dungeon.

Now celebrate in the king's court

The food grown at the farm makes
a magnificent victory feast!

Tall chair

Column base

1

2

3

4

5

6

7

8

| 1 | 3 |
| 2 | 4 |

x2

9

1	3
2	4
	5

x2

10

11

12

x2

Table with cheese

Candle sconce

About Sean

Sean Kenney likes to prove you can build anything with LEGO bricks. He makes sculptures and models all day at his studio in New York City and is recognized as one of the premier LEGO brick builders in the world.

Visit Sean at seankenney.com to:

- Share your cool castle creations with kids around the world
- Order some extra LEGO pieces
- See more cool castle creations
- Find out if Sean is coming to your neighborhood . . . and more!